ASIA

Red Ant
(lives in many places on Earth)

Beluga Sturgeon

Japanese Spider Crab

Chinese Giant Salamander

Bumblebee Bat

Dwarf Goby

AFRICA

Queen Alexandra's Birdwing

African Elephant

INDIAN OCEAN

AUSTRALIA

Fairy Shrimp
(lives in many places on Earth)

WHERE CREATURES LIVE

ANTARCTICA

CREATURES
Great and Small

KAREN PATKAU

TUNDRA BOOKS

Published in Canada by Tundra Books,
75 Sherbourne Street, Toronto, Ontario M5A 2P9

Published in the United States by Tundra Books of Northern New York,
P.O. Box 1030, Plattsburgh, New York 12901

Library of Congress Control Number: 2005910625

Library and Archives Canada Cataloguing in Publication

Patkau, Karen
    Creatures great and small / Karen Patkau.

ISBN-13: 978-0-88776-754-8
ISBN-10: 0-88776-754-0

    1. Animals – Juvenile literature. 2. Body size – Juvenile literature.
I. Title.

QL49.P38 2006   j591.4'1   C2005-907309-8

We acknowledge the financial support of the Government of Canada
through the Book Publishing Industry Development Program (BPIDP) and
that of the Government of Ontario through the Ontario Media
Development Corporation's Ontario Book Initiative.
We further acknowledge the support of the Canada Council for the Arts
and the Ontario Arts Council for our publishing program.

ONTARIO ARTS COUNCIL
CONSEIL DES ARTS DE L'ONTARIO

Medium: Digital

Printed in Hong Kong, China

1 2 3 4 5 6   11 10 09 08 07 06

To my mother.

With special thanks to Michael Kacsor, James Wilson,

Diane Fine, and Dr. Jane Berg.

CREATURES GREAT

Blue Whale

I am the largest animal. Did you know I am the loudest one, too? I swim deep in oceans, around the world. I come to the surface to breathe.

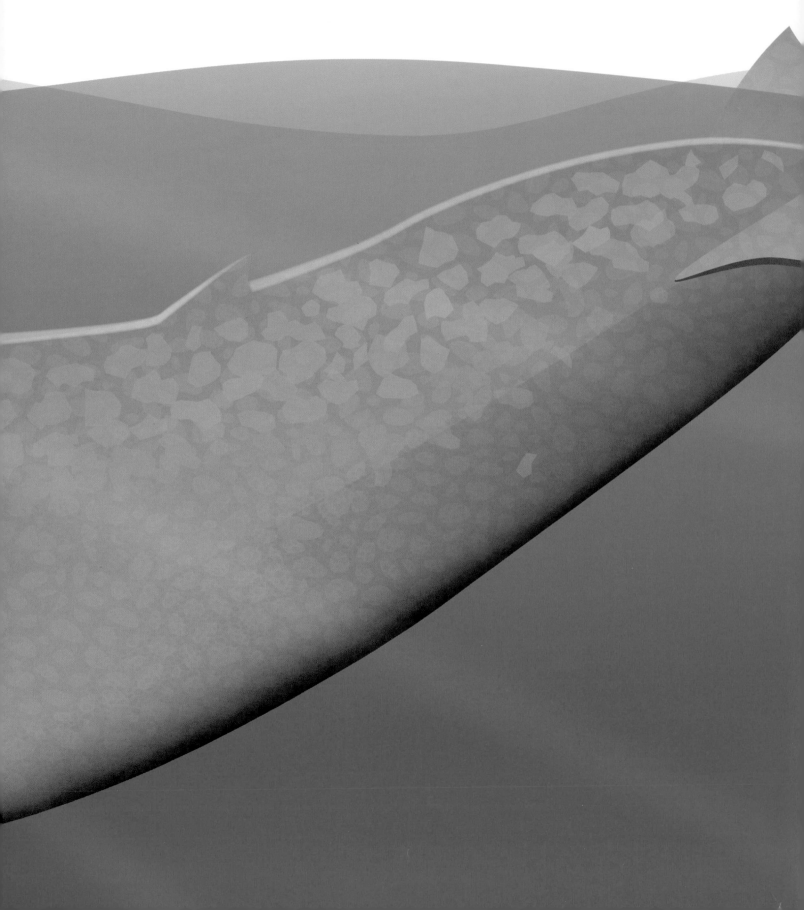

AND SMALL

Red Ant

I am little, but very strong. You can find me on land, almost anywhere on Earth. I live with a large ant colony, in an anthill or a rotting tree. Hard at work, I scurry about.

INSECTS

Queen Alexandra's Birdwing

I am a butterfly, not a moth. I am active in the daytime and flutter about the jungle. Landing on flowers, I sip their nectar through my strawlike proboscis.

Feather-Winged Beetle

I have four wings. The front two shield the back two, which are for flying. I have six legs and like to crawl under tree bark in the woods. I also like to eat fungus.

FISH

Beluga Sturgeon

Call me a living fossil – I can live for one hundred years. With rows of bony scutes to protect my sides, I cruise in salt water. I migrate up a river to spawn.

Dwarf Goby

Even though I am almost transparent, can you spy my little eye in this freshwater stream? Because I have no eyelids, my eyes are always open. Even while I sleep!

MAMMALS

African Elephant
My trunk sways as I stride across the land.
I use it to touch and grasp, as well as to
suck and breathe. With ears like big fans,
I can keep cool. My hearing is excellent.

Bumblebee Bat

Inside a damp cave, I hang upside down by my feet. My wings are long fingers covered in skin. Swooping through the sky at night, I use echolocation to find my way.

SEA JELLIES

Arctic Lion's Mane
My body is like an umbrella. I have no brain, heart, bones, or blood. As I drift in ocean currents, my long tentacles trail far behind me. They sting anything they touch.

Thimble Jellyfish

Neither a thimble nor a fish, I jiggle and bob in the warm salty sea. In fact, I am made mostly of water. If I wash up onto a hot sunny beach, I dry up.

REPTILES

Anaconda

I sun myself high in a tree, or slither through a swamp on the hunt. Winding my body around my prey, I squeeze it tightly. Then I swallow it whole and feel full for weeks.

Dwarf Gecko

I dart all about my island home on gripping, padded toes. I go everywhere, even upside down. If you catch me by the tail, it drops off and I escape. Later, it grows back.

AMPHIBIANS

Chinese Giant Salamander

I live in the mountains, among the rocks of muddy riverbanks. Nocturnal, I am awake at night. That is when I crawl along the cold riverbed, searching for a meal.

Poison Dart Frog

I hop among leaves on the rain-forest floor.
I catch insects with my long sticky tongue.
If you see me, watch out! My bright,
slippery skin is deadly, if you touch it.

BIRDS

Ostrich

See me dash across the savanna. I am the fastest living thing on two legs. Although I have splendid wings, I cannot fly. I wander in search of plants and bushes to eat.

Bee Hummingbird

Hear my wings *hummmm* as I fly. I am an acrobat in the air. I hover to drink nectar from tropical flowers. Diving at intruders, I charge them with my sharp beak.

CRUSTACEANS

Japanese Spider Crab

I amble along the ocean floor, scooping up food as I go. To defend myself, I pinch with my sharp front claws. Sometimes, I attach sponges to my shell for camouflage.

Fairy Shrimp

You can find me in pools of rainwater. Belly-side-up, I like to make waves with my twenty-two swimmerets. When a pool dries up, my eggs lie dormant, until it rains again.

ARACHNIDS

Goliath Tarantula

A hairy, eight-eyed spider, I keep snug
and warm in my underground burrow.
When I get ready to pounce – look out!
I will bite you with my venomous fangs.

Rocky Mountain Wood Tick

An eight-legged parasite, I cannot run, hop, or fly. Instead, I perch at the top of a stem or blade of grass and wait for an animal to come by. I latch on to it and suck its blood.

MOLLUSKS

Giant Squid
Squirting water through a siphon, I propel myself through the sea. I have eight arms with suckers and two feeding tentacles. I eat with a beak and breathe with gills.

Garden Snail

I bury myself in the dirt, but come out in damp weather. A hard shell protects my soft body. Sliding slowly along on one broad foot, I leave a slimy trail.

SIZE

Units of Measure

1 m (meter) = 3.28 ft. (feet)

1 ft. (foot) = .31 m (meters)

African Elephant
3.9 m / 13 ft. tall

Human
1.86 m / 6 ft. tall

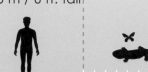

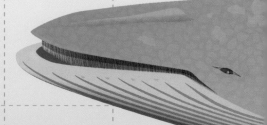

Blue Whale
30.5 m / 100 ft. long

Big

1 grid square = .31 meters or 1 foot

Queen Alexandra's Birdwing
.31 m / 1 ft. wide

Goliath Tarantula
.31 m / 1 ft. wide

Chinese Giant Salamander
1.5 m / 5 ft. long

Really Big

1 grid square = 3.1 meters or 10 feet

Japanese Spider Crab
3.7 m / 12 ft. wide

Anaconda
11 m / 36 ft. long

Ostrich
2.7 m / 9 ft. tall

Giant Squid
18 m / 59 ft. long

Beluga Sturgeon
7.6 m / 25 ft. long

Arctic Lion's Mane
45.8 m / 150 ft. long

SIZE

Units of Measure

1 cm (centimeter) = .39 in. (inches)

1 in. (inch) = 2.54 cm (centimeters)

1 in. (inch) = 25.4 mm (millimeters)

1 cm (centimeter) = 10 mm (millimeters)

1 mm (millimeter) = .04 in. (inches)

Actual Size

Small

2 x Actual Size

Thimble Jellyfish
1.5 cm / .59 in. long

2 x Actual Size

Dwarf Gecko
1.6 cm / .62 in. long

2 x Actual Size

Garden Snail
2 cm / .78 in. long

3 x Actual Size

Fairy Shrimp
1.3 cm / .51 in. long

3 x Actual Size

Poison Dart Frog
1.3 cm / .51 in. long

Actual Size

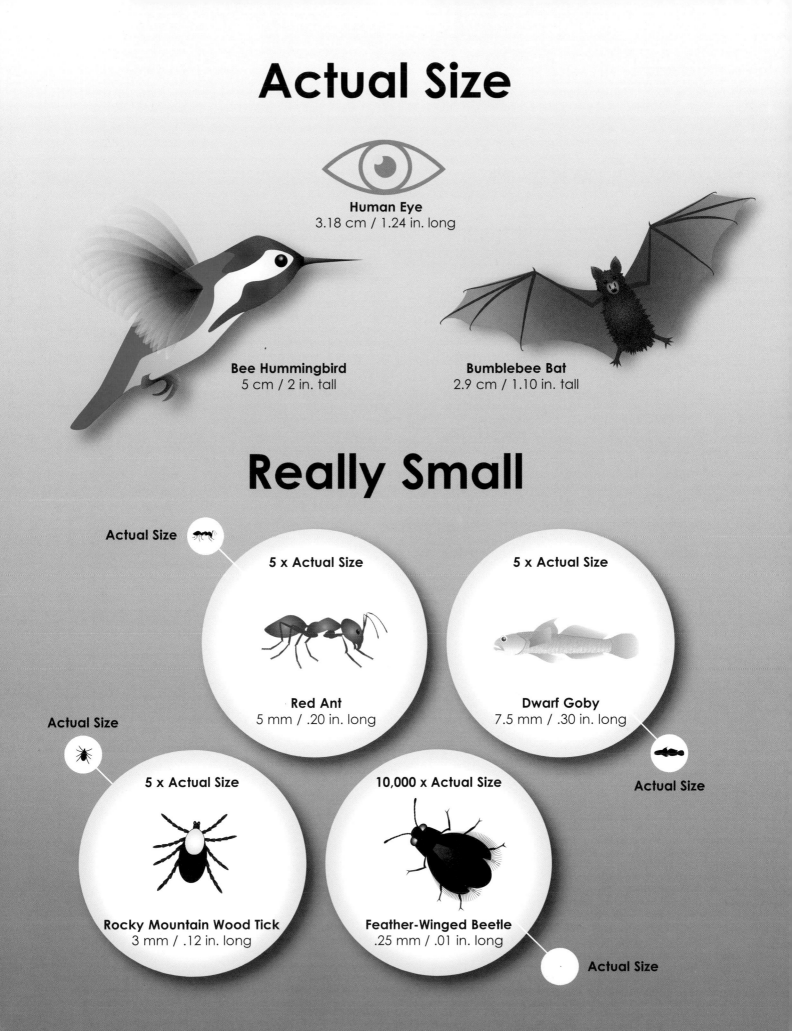

Human Eye
3.18 cm / 1.24 in. long

Bee Hummingbird
5 cm / 2 in. tall

Bumblebee Bat
2.9 cm / 1.10 in. tall

Really Small

Actual Size

5 x Actual Size

Red Ant
5 mm / .20 in. long

5 x Actual Size

Dwarf Goby
7.5 mm / .30 in. long

Actual Size

Actual Size

5 x Actual Size

Rocky Mountain Wood Tick
3 mm / .12 in. long

10,000 x Actual Size

Feather-Winged Beetle
.25 mm / .01 in. long

Actual Size

GLOSSARY

camouflage – a disguise to make something appear as part of its surroundings

colony – a group of the same kind of animals that live together

creature – an animal or living being

dormant – being inactive or asleep

echolocation – a process for locating objects by reflected sound

fungus – a parasitic nongreen plant in the same group as the mushroom

migrate – to seasonally move from one place to another for feeding or breeding

nocturnal – being active at night

parasite – one animal living in, with, or off another, but giving nothing in return

prey – an animal that is hunted by another animal for food

proboscis – a long slender tube used for sucking up food

propel – to push forward or cause to move

savanna – a flat dry grassland

scutes – tough external plates or large scales

siphon – a tube through which liquid is taken in or forced out

spawn – to produce eggs or offspring, especially in large numbers

swimmerets – small paddlelike limbs used for swimming

tentacles – long flexible feelers

transparent – clear enough to be seen through

venomous – capable of injuring or killing by injecting poison

ARCTIC OCEAN

Rocky
Mountain
Wood Tick

NORTH
AMERICA

Feather-Winged Beetle
(lives in many places on Earth)

• Arctic Lion's Mane

Garden Snail
(lives in many
places on Earth)

EUROPE

• Thimble Jellyfish

• Bee Hummingbird

Ostrich

• Dwarf Gecko

DISCARD

• Giant Squid

Anaconda

PACIFIC OCEAN

IC OCEAN

Blue Whale
(swims in oceans all around